The Power to BELIEVE

For: _____

Dated: _____

I BELIEVE...

...in your worth, in the value it adds to others,
and the value it gives to You, and your
CONFIDENCE TO BELIEVE.

...That tomorrow is a chance to Begin Again,
that failures are the stepping stones to Greatness,
OPPORTUNITIES FOR THOSE WHO BELIEVE.

...That compassion is in the giving of Love and Appreciation,
with an open heart and mind, a feeling of connection to your higher self.
A POWERFUL FORCE TO BELIEVE.

...In your Faith, Family and Friends, the most important people in your life.
They are Angels that lift us to our feet, give us wings to fly, and the
FAITH TO BELIEVE.

...In Your Greatness, to inspire your Dreams and Desires, knowing
ALL THINGS ARE POSSIBLE FOR THOSE WHO BELIEVE.

...that you deserve the Best Life and You Do Make A Difference!
There is something Magnificent about You
that shines through everything You Do...
IT'S TIME TO IGNITE THE POWER IN YOU!

Melanie A. Brown

*If you don't have the power to Believe,
take my belief in You, and Make Your Life Shine!*

Surround yourself with the *Dreamers* and the *Doers*, the *Believers* and the *Thinkers*, but most of all, surround yourself with those who see the *Greatness* within *You*, even when you don't see it yourself.

edmundslee.com

This is the beginning of a New Life...

Make every day a masterpiece.

What did I do today to Make a Difference...

BELIEVE

I am so Happy and Grateful for...

Tell a Friend why they mean the world to you...

What am I doing to build my Confidence to Believe...

BELIEVE

You have the power...

Let your confidence Shine...

Confidence will always lead you to the next best step...

BELIEVE

Become an Aspiring Leader...

Every day is an Opportunity...

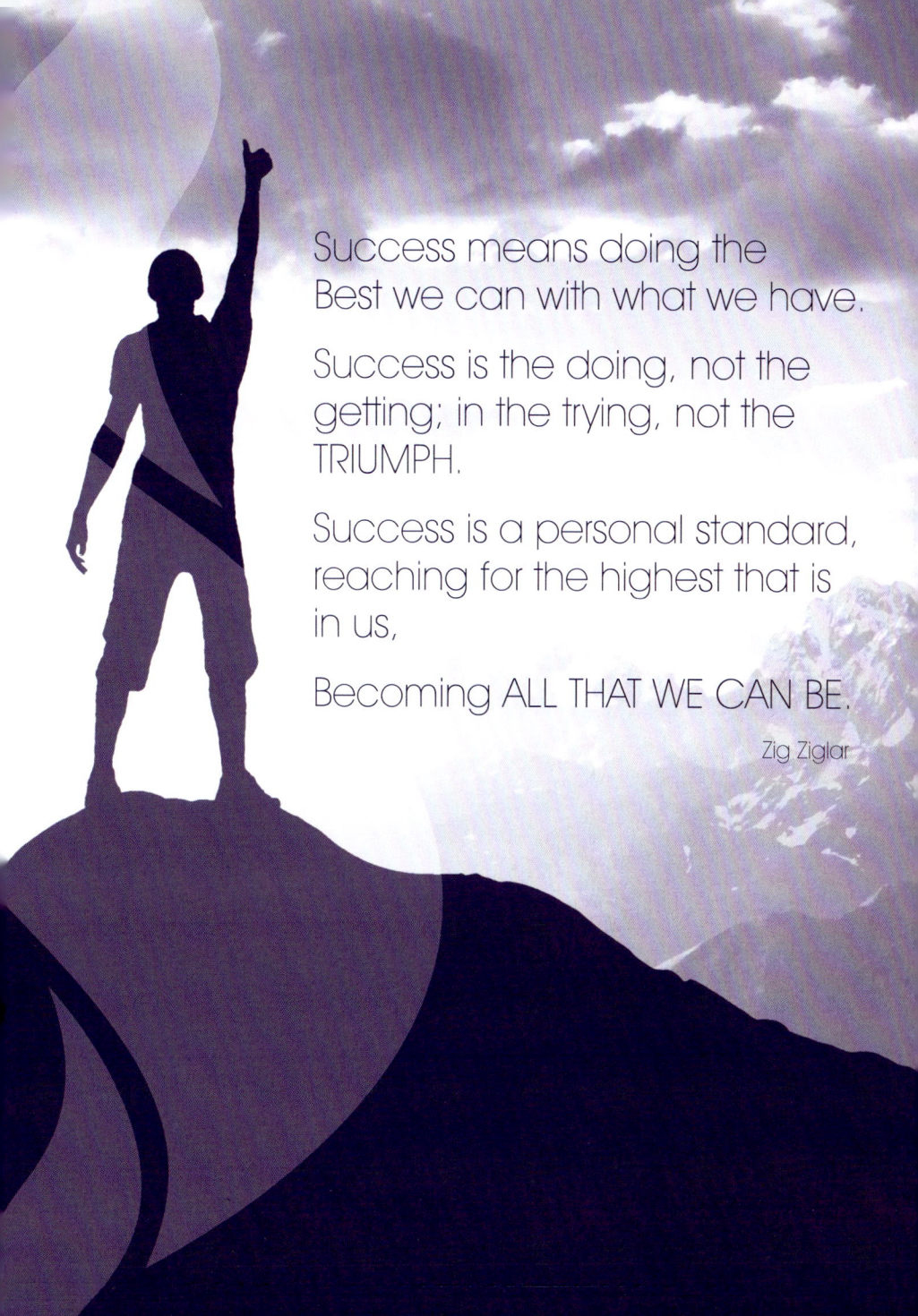

Today Inspire and Motivate those around you...

Be someone's Miracle today...

Look for ways to
Reach out and
Make
a
Difference...

BELIEVE

Create an Encouragement File...

Give encouragement to everyone around you…

Choose the
Voice
of Victory...

BELIEVE

Find your strength zone...

Give Fear the Failure.

Give
Hugs away
all day.

BELIEVE

The Leadership starts within...

then Lead out...

If an egg is
broken by
Outside Force,
Life Ends.
If broken by
Inside Force,
Life Begins.
Great things always
begin from Inside.

Jim Kwik

BELIEVE

Change your
Thinking...

Change Your Life.

Let Everyone else
go first today
And watch
what
Happens...

BELIEVE

Decide it will Happen...

Give to the community, serve food at the Food Bank.

Align your priorities, they make your life shine.

BELIEVE

That's Life...
FAITH IT...

Encourage Yourself...

I will manage my time more effectively...

BELIEVE

You've got to think high to Rise.

Be the Winner!

SUCCESS HABITS

Before you Pray
Believe

Before you Speak
Listen

Before you Spend
Earn

Before you Write
Think

Before you Quit
Try and. . .

Before you Die
Live!

Dave Sommers

Take time to show you CARE...

Be Your Best Every day.

I am so
Happy and
Grateful for...

BELIEVE

Compliment... Compliment... Compliment...

Live with no regrets.

Nothing You Do
for Children
is ever wasted.

BELIEVE

What do you love to Do...

Zip up the Doubt.

Your greatest
victories
are still out there.

BELIEVE

Make today SHINE...

Be the Light for someone else.

Today I am so Grateful
that God knows my Heart.
Others may misunderstand
my good intentions,
judge my words or deeds,
Find fault, or blame what they
truly don't understand.

But God knows my Heart.
He knows I am learning,
trying, endeavoring,
To Be All He Created Me To BE.

Lori Nawyn

BELIEVE

What decisions can I make today that will **forever** change my Life...

Remember to always Pray.

Leave the change
at the checkout
Counter for
someone
else to find.

BELIEVE

Make today
Magnificent.

Smile just Because.

I will
Praise and Raise,
Not complain
and remain.

BELIEVE

DREAM BIGGER...

Just say "YES" to Life.

Nothing is Impossible. The word says I'M POSSIBLE.

BELIEVE

I am so Happy and Grateful for...

_____
_____
_____
_____
_____
_____
_____
_____
_____
_____
_____
_____
_____
_____
_____
_____
_____

Thank You...

Enthusiasm is one of the most powerful engines of Success. When you do a thing, do it with all your might. Put your whole soul into it. Stamp it with your own personality. Be active, be energetic, be enthusiastic, and faithful, and you will accomplish your object. Nothing great was ever achieved without Enthusiasm.

Ralph Waldo Emerson

Choose Your own Dream Team...

It's Your Time!

Always offer
to do someone
a Favor...

BELIEVE

Try it One More Time...

Never Give Up!

Look for the
Powerful Change
that can be created
from the
Challenge.

BELIEVE

Capture Your Ideas...

Be quick to Apologize.

Clean out your closet and give to Charity,
De-clutter your life.

BELIEVE

Give Fear the
Failure...

Rise Above.

FEAR
has two meanings:

Forget **E**verything **A**nd **R**un

or

Faith **E**verything **A**nd **R**ise

The Choice is Yours!

BELIEVE

Realize Your
Potential...

Stay Determined.

Every job is a self-portrait of the person who did it. Autograph your work with excellence.

Vince Lombardi

BELIEVE

Look for ways to **lighten** someone else's **load**...

Be a Burden Lifter.

Always have an
Attitude
of Gratitude...

BELIEVE

Stay true to your Heart...

Be an Original.

Don't allow that critical spirit to come out.

BELIEVE

Surround Yourself with Greatness...

Be a People Builder.

Start showing the world your **Inner Winner**, and toss away for good The Outer Doubter.

Jennifer Gayle

Add value to others daily...

Open the door to generosity.

The best way
to find yourself
is to lose
yourself in the
service
   of others.

Ghandi

BELIEVE

Take time
to laugh and play...

Child's play is serious learning.

Laughing is Soul Food.

BELIEVE

Forgive to Live...

Send a note to say "I'm Sorry."

Refresh and renew Yourself, your Body Mind and Spirit.

BELIEVE

Abundance is your Birthright.

Expect the Best.

A Good Life is when you assume nothing

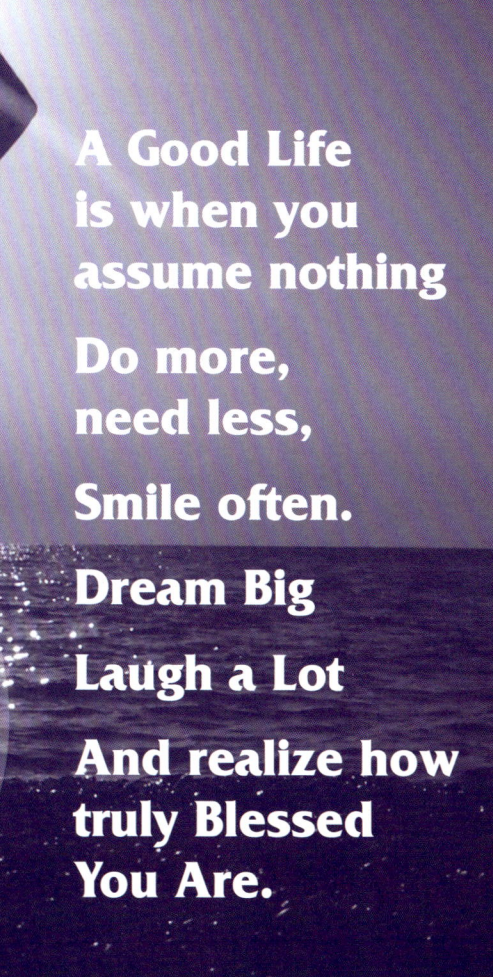

Do more, need less,

Smile often.

Dream Big

Laugh a Lot

And realize how truly Blessed You Are.

BELIEVE

Begin Again...

What miracle did I create today...

PAUSE
and enjoy the
Moment.

BELIEVE

Believe You Can...

*Take time to
add money to an expired meter.*

Leave someone a note to "Have a great day." It will definitely make yours.

BELIEVE

I am so Happy and Grateful for...

Give a Smile to every stranger you meet.

Never go to
bed until you
say "I Love You"
to someone.

BELIEVE

It's time to Treat Yourself...

Enjoy Sweetness.

Laugh until your body aches.

Cry until you start to shake.

Live like the world is yours to take.

And love as though your heart won't break.

I **love** today because...

Do It Now...Make It Happen.

Wake Up
15 minutes
earlier
And watch what
happens.

BELIEVE

I am so Happy and Grateful for...

Buy extra canned goods to donate.

Today is your
day. Make it Special.

BELIEVE

I promise to
get better AT...

Wish everyone you meet a Great Day.

What can I do
Differently
to get
Better results...

BELIEVE

Accept yourself and realize how truly **Amazing** you really are...

Be Brilliant.

You must
find the
place inside
yourself,
Where nothing
is Impossible.
Deepak Chopra
BELIEVE

I am so Happy and Grateful for...

Today I am going to go the extra mile.

Make a difference in your community: Volunteer.

BELIEVE

Dare to Dream a New Dream...

Have calm confidence.

Be Awesome Today...

BELIEVE

Never Give Up...

Follow Your Intuition.

Determination
Wins the race.

BELIEVE

Celebrate
everything that happened...

Cheers to Your Success & Brilliance~

People are often unreasonable and self-centered. Forgive them anyway.
If you are kind, people may accuse you of ulterior motives. Be kind anyway.
If you are honest, people may cheat you. Be honest anyway.
If you find happiness, people may be jealous. Be happy anyway.
The good you do today, may be forgotten tomorrow. Do good anyway.
Give the world the best you have, and it may never be enough.
Give your best anyway!

Mother Teresa

I am so Happy and Grateful for...

Never wait...Do It Now.

Celebrate the little
things in life
And you will
find a reason to
Celebrate
Every day.

BELIEVE

Stay Inspired...

Live in your strength zone.

Let your inner critic
Become
your inner Coach.

BELIEVE

Forgive
them anyway...

It's never too late.

Believe Big
and
Dare to Fail.

BELIEVE

Give your Best anyway...

You Deserve It!

With every Sunrise, We are Born all over again. The power of a fresh start is ours for the taking, With the Simple Choice to BEGIN AGAIN.

BELIEVE

I am so Happy and Grateful for...

Embrace Your Greatness.

Perform much...
Accomplish Much.

BELIEVE

It will happen because of **your Actions...**

Make Date Night a weekly Celebration.

Start where You Are.

BELIEVE

Open your Gifts...

Pursue what captures your Heart.

It's time to
Begin Again.

BELIEVE

Dream It...
Dare It...

Believe In Yourself.

Always believe in **YOU**.

Listen to your heart.

Trust your instincts.

Know you **CAN**.

See your own strengths.

Dream It…Dare It.

DO what you are afraid of.

Keep the Faith.

Follow Your Vision.

Remember, **Anything** is possible if only YOU BELIEVE!

# Make it a
Great Day...

I am so Blessed.

Listen closely
to your heart;
it knows the
way.

BELIEVE

I am so Happy and Grateful for...

Don't be in a hurry.

Expose yourself to
your deepest Fear.
Dream through IT.

BELIEVE

That's Life...
FAITH IT...

Follow Your Vision.

Limitations are overcome by Imagination.

BELIEVE

Anything is possible
If only you Believe.

Never stop Believing.

The most basic and powerful way to connect to another person is to listen. Just listen.

Perhaps the most important thing we ever give each other is our attention.

A loving silence often has far more power to heal and to connect than the most well-intentioned words.

BELIEVE

Dare to Believe in You...

Make a Difference!

Empower your
Confidence
that lies deep
Inside.

BELIEVE

Inspired Thoughts...

Let your faith Lead the Way.

Embrace your
Vision
Believe there are
No Limits.

BELIEVE

IGNITE
The Power in You